CÉSAR FRANCK

Symphony in D Minor

IN FULL SCORE

Dover Publications, Inc., New York

Published in Canada by General Publishing Company, Ltd.,
30 Lesmill Road, Don Mills, Toronto, Ontario.
Published in the United Kingdom by Constable and Company, Ltd.

This Dover edition, first published in 1987,
is an unaltered and unabridged republication of
Symphonie pour Orchestre par César Franck
as published by J. Hamelle, Paris, n.d.

Manufactured in the United States of America
Dover Publications, Inc., 31 East 2nd Street, Mineola, N.Y. 11501

Library of Congress Cataloging-in-Publication Data

Franck, César, 1822–1890.
[Symphony, D minor]
Symphony in D minor.

"Opus [i.e. M.] 48"—P.
Reprint. Originally published: Symphonie pour
orchestre. Paris : Hamelle, 189–.
1. Symphonies—Scores.   I. Title.
M1001.F822   Op. 48   1987   86-755095
ISBN 0-486-25373-2

Symphony in D Minor

(Opus 48, composed 1886–88; dedicated "to my friend Henri Duparc")

Glossary of French Terms
in the Score

changez . . . en . . . : change . . . to . . .
double corde: double stopping
fa: F
la: A
la moitié des . . . : half of the . . .
largement: broadly
*les temps de même valeur (*OR: *les temps ont exactement la même valeur):* the change of meter does not affect the tempo (♩ = ♪)
mettez les sourdines: attach the mutes

ôtez les sourdines: remove the mutes
ré: D
si: B
sol: G
toujours à 2: continuing "a 2"
toujours la même valeur aux temps: maintain a constant tempo despite change in meter
tous: all
très long: very long
ut: C

Instrumentation

2 Flûtes (Flutes); 2 Hautbois (Oboes); Cor anglais (English Horn); 2 Clarinettes en si♭ (B-flat Clarinets); Clarinette basse en si♭ (Bass Clarinet in B-flat); 2 Bassons (Bassoons).

4 Cors chrom[atiques] en fa (Horns in F); 2 Trompettes en fa (Trumpets in F); 2 Cornets à pist[on] en si♭ (Cornets in B-flat); 3 Trombones; Tuba.

Timbales (Kettledrums).

Harpes (Harps).

1rs & 2ds Violons (Violins I & II); Altos (Violas); Violoncelles (Celli); Contrebasses (Double Basses).

I.

3

4

7

changer la en sol, ré en si♭ et fa en ré

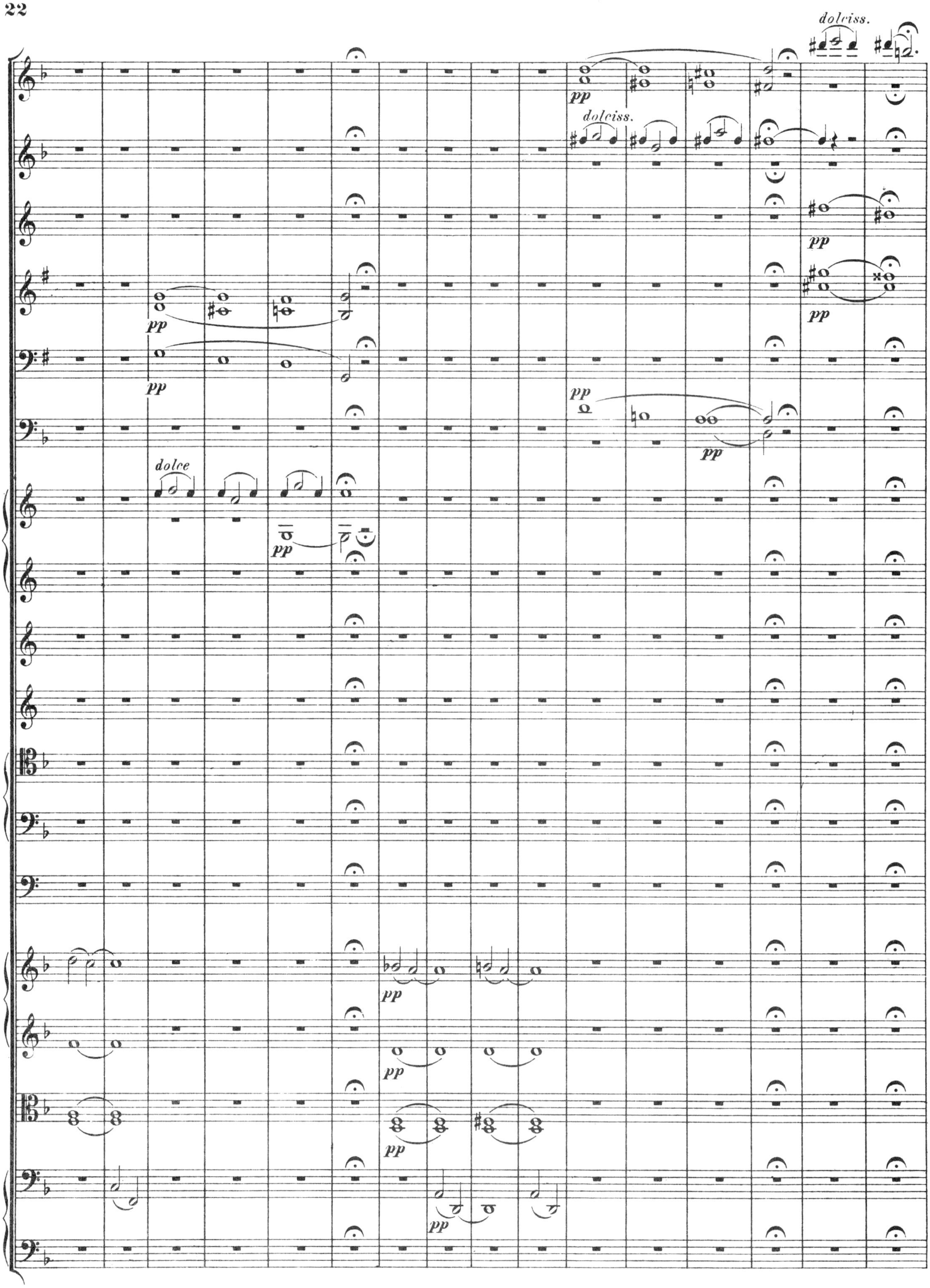
dolciss.
pp
dolciss.
pp
pp
pp
pp
pp
pp
dolce
pp
pp
pp
pp
pp

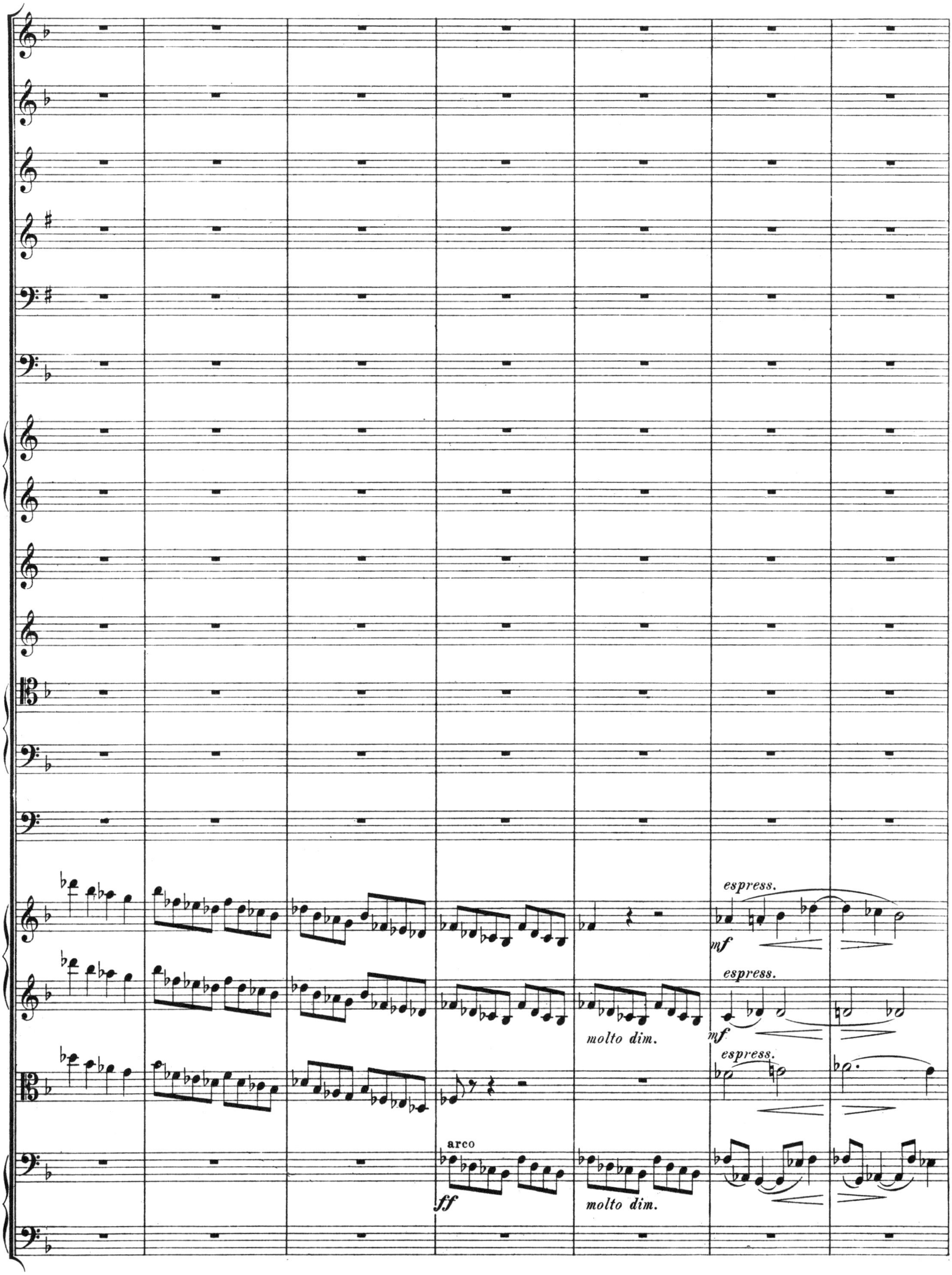
espress.
mf
espress.
molto dim.
mf
espress.
arco
ff
molto dim.

Lento.

changez si♭ en si♮

Lento.

Lento.

Allegro.

61

II.

B

B

dolce espress.

arco

arco

arco

III.

114

Les temps ont exactement la même valeur.

Les temps ont exactement la même valeur.

Les temps ont exactement la même valeur.

Les temps ont toujours la même valeur.

Les temps ont toujours la même valeur.

Les temps ont toujours la même valeur.

118

changer la ♭ en sol

Tempo I. Allegro non troppo.

changer sol en la

Tempo I. Allegro non troppo.

Tempo I. Allegro non troppo.